Wild Domestic

ALSO BY TAMARA MADISON

The Belly Remembers

TAMARA MADISON

Wild Domestic

Pearl
Editions
LONG BEACH, CALIFORNIA

Library of Congress Control Number: 2011924012

Copyright © 2011 by Tamara Madison
All Rights Reserved
Printed in the United States of America

ISBN 978-1-888219-39-5

Book design by Marilyn Johnson

Cover photo: "Condo" by A.J. Ford. © 1993

This publisher is a proud member of

[clmp]

COUNCIL OF LITERARY MAGAZINES & PRESSES
W W W . C L M P . O R G

PEARL EDITIONS
3030 E. Second Street
Long Beach, California 90803

www.pearlmag.com

To my mother, of course, and Shaligram

ACKNOWLEDGMENTS

I would like to thank the editors of the magazines in which the following poems first appeared:

Beggars & Cheeseburgers: "Circe Plans," "The Norman Invasion," "One," "The Streak"

Chiron Review: "Acceptance Speech," "Big Dick," "The Body of God," "Done," "Drop Dead," "I've Had Tits," "Lay," "The Return of the Subjunctive"

The Eldorado Poetry Review: "Your Ocean"

Pearl: "Impasse," "Malibu Fire," "Wild Domestic"

Shelia-Na-Gig: "On the Loss of an Only Child"

Tears in the Fence: "The Snow Trip"

A number of poems in this volume also appeared in the chapbook, *The Belly Remembers*, and in a featured section of *Pearl 43*.

I would also like to thank all my friends and family and everyone I know for giving me inspiration, with special thanks to everyone in Donna Hilbert's poetry workshop.

CONTENTS

V. The Radiance

Ultra Deep Field

SEQUOIA SEMPERVIRENS

Some of these trees have been here
since Jesus walked on water
Some of these trees have been here
since Vikings drove their boats
onto the shores of Newfoundland
Some of these trees were seedlings
while the Mayans were worshiping time
while the dire wolf and saber-toothed
tiger roamed North America
Some of these trees have survived
lightning strikes and forest fires
Some of these trees house creatures
of the forest floor in burned-out caves
at the base of their ruddy trunks
Some of these trees have become
living pipes, chimneys, hollowed out
by fire. They have grown beyond
their trauma and focus now
on the daily climb, the adding-on
of needle and bark, on nature's drive
to rise above and see beyond
until the day when death will fell them
and the earth will add them to its riches.
We can be like these trees, pull on
the layers of living like fine
new garments, house the needy
in the caverns of our grief, grow
beyond the stories of our scars
stretch our branches toward
the bristling stars.

ANALOG TIME

Your new watch can tell
what time it is right down
to the second, the split second.
Your new watch has no face;
instead there's a blinking grill
where the numbers change
constantly. I would like to say
that in this rapid split-second
parade we can see the flow
of time—always changing,
never changing, a river slipping
over rocks and sand—but it's
only time, a human concept
after all, not a real river.
Your new watch honors
each second by giving it
its own number which tumbles
swiftly away, anchoring us,
if we let it, in Now.

Still I prefer the grace
of the analog clock
with its face, its hands,
where every moment
is linked to those around it:
each moment has a history
and a future, where it's
ten past the hour, half past,
a quarter till, five of, as though
each moment is truly part
of a fluid whole. But in fact
the real tellers of time
are the sun, the sky,
the wrinkles on our faces,
the bruises on our souls.

ULTRA DEEP FIELD
Note from Lover Number 403

These photons traveled 13 billion years
So you could see them on your laptop screen
Ten thousand blips of light, each one
A galaxy in its own right, each one only

One of the hundred billion galaxies
In the universe. All around us
What we're sure is empty is actually full:
This glass of water, for example—

Teeming with organisms I'm glad
I can't see. The hair you left on my pillow—
Full of tiny creatures I can't make out
With my naked eye. Your smile—

Full of experiences you had before me.
Your greeting—more full of lies than a pack
Of lawmakers. When I peer into your
Ultra deep field, how many galaxies

Of one-night-stands will I see sprinkled
Among your handfuls of romances
That lasted for more than one year,
Never more than two? Ah fair one,

I am closing my telescope now and my
Microscope too, to return to the well-worn
Minutiae of my own life's cozy galaxy.

THE MOUNTAIN

My child sleeps on her stomach;
one arm crawls over her head
like a swimmer's,
mouth with lush lips
open, a constellation
of moles on her shoulder,
stray stars flung
about the rest of her.
Her breath is a spring breeze
moving curtains, one lock
of hair curls up from her earlobe
to lick the new, rose-lit
earring. With many rings,
bracelets of plastic lace,
I watch her gaily skirt the foothills
of adolescence, just poised
to make the climb; still
the mountain looms
and she sleeps
in its deep green shadow.

FALLS

My son stands at boulder's edge
deep water stares up shimmering
in the push of the falls.

Don't dive, I say, please,
you don't dive into black water
with rocks all around!

We have seen the others jump,
tuck heels under hips, fly
over the rocks, into the ink.
No, he promises, he won't dive.

But when he finally leaps from the rock,
he arcs—head first—like an arrow,
pierces the rock pool's glistening face.
Water closes black over him.
I die in that dark moment.

The man who jumped
from the Trade Center tower
might have shot himself
just like that
into the still clear air
before falling into that casual pose,
one knee up as if marching
down the sun-bright vertical
windows.

I see my child's head crown through
the water's under side, face born anew
in a rush of bubbles
and I see once more
the smile that burst
like a sun atop the red bike's
first unsteady loop.

Vile child! I want to cry
but can't deny his joy. Instead I plant
my own feet on the granite shoulder,
raise arms above my head,
take aim at the dark mirror.

KEYS
Big Sur, California

In the photo my children
run along a wet shoreline
on a bright day of whipping winds.
Jagged cliffs of red stone and gray
rise like bleachers
above the flinging sand.

He is the young man in baggy shorts
and sunglasses, hair flying,
grinning wide as he runs,
leggy sister on his back.
Her hood tied round her face
is like a mouth pronouncing "cow,"
but you can see in the narrow patch
of light that shows only a peek of nose,
the inner corners of eyes, a touch
of upper lip, that she is grinning too.
Her legs dangling through his pocketed arms
are bare, strong-calved in blue gym shoes.

He has not yet climbed
the rocky island that rises unseen
behind them in the greenwhite frothing
surf, and I do not yet know
that my keys lie somewhere hidden
beneath the blowing sand,
that it will take an hour of worry,
the help of strangers, and finally,
an unbeliever's desperate plea
to Saint Anthony before the wind
will part the sand to reveal them,
the keys to everything else
that seems important in my life.

THE BOSS

When The Boss drives onto the lot
it's like winter arriving
in a rush of frost: backs stiffen
conversation stops and everyone
returns to their places braced
for the latest onslaught, this day's
announcement of which goddamned
idiot did the stupid thing.

It's the same at home: the door slams
the windows shake and everyone
tries to look the right kind of busy.
But at home there's the glass of scotch
and a snack. You know it's safe
to talk again when he glowers
from the doorway with his tumbler
and a slice of Black Diamond to proclaim:
"This is the BEST cheese!"
and no one dares to contradict.

After the strokes you still tread softly
but it's different now, you're afraid
to see the sudden tear, the bewilderment.
One morning his hunched back turns
from Mr. Rogers, he looks up into your face
to tell you, "That is the NICEST man!"
You want to hold him then, the little boy
who never got held enough, but then
you remember The Boss.

EXPERT MARKSMAN

The army ranked him Expert Marksman
But he didn't like to shoot.
Shot over the heads of some German kids—
Candy stealers—when the war was over,
Shot to scare off some coyotes hounding
Our dog in the field down below the house,
And once when a strange rustling
Disturbed our sleep for the third night in a row
His shot fired into the dark turned up a badger.
Otherwise, the shotgun stood unloaded
In a dark corner of my parents' closet.

Once a friend's kid beebee'd down a bird
And my dad told him the whole story
Of that young bird's life, how just that morning,
That bird was singing, riding the April breezes
Gathering up food for its babies; he went on
Until the kid melted into a blubbering mass.

When his pals took him hunting
He told them he was only along for the ride,
He didn't believe in killing. But he hefted
The rifle they handed him and aimed
Without thinking toward the rustling brush.
He was the only one to get a deer that trip,
And when he came home he cried, telling about it.

When Bullet was twelve and couldn't jump
Into the pickup bed, could hardly hobble
Out to greet his master, when his dog smile
Darkened with pain, my father came home
One day, took off his hat but wouldn't take
His eye off the ground: he just couldn't stand
To see the dog in pain like that.

DADDY'S BELLY

Daddy's belly
boulder big
round brown drum
slick with sweat
He'd come up
to the house
for dinner
when the sun was high
smell of metal
smell of weed oil
smell of cold aluminum
beer
I'd sit next to him
at the eating bar
to watch him eat
the sandwich
dripping lettuce
the steak
bathed in gravy
I was there to watch
his big brown belly
the fork a tiny tool
in leathery hand
the wrinkled elbow
tough and brown
like the hardened end
of my baked potato

SNOW TRIP

We drive the winding road
up the mountain to the snow
and watch my father draw
a big circle in a clearing.
He shows my friend and me
a game about rabbits and a fox,
runs around like a ten-year-old;
frost hangs from his breath.
We shout run chase each other
fall in the snow tumble all white
wet and amazed that my stern
and dour father can play
so high and wild, and fun.

In the car on the way home,
clothes wet, giddy with winter
and the treasure of finding
in my father this amazing playmate,
my friend and I giggle and shriek
in the back seat, louder and louder
until our new pal, transformed
into hairy-eyed ogre, whips
his head toward the back seat:
> "If you two don't shut your traps
> I'll pinch you till you bleed!"

With no effort now we fall silent.
Trees careen past, shaking snow;
the ground turns red; pines become
mesquite, shimmery winter woods
become desert, the road spins
down the mountain like a serpent's tail
and I know I have seen
something I will never see again.

WE USE HIM

I stood by the bed
the day my father died,
holding his hand,
feeling the thin tremble
of his pulse
with my fingertips.

He was yellow,
breathing faintly
but he knew we were there
for his eyes flickered,
his head nodded,
he was waiting for us.
He seemed to look up
with his eyelids
and then fall, relieved,
into death's cool hand.

Now we use him.
My son walks on his legs.
My sister throws his shadow
across the pool.
My brother wears
his burnished, bald crown.
His eyes regard me
from the mirror,
and when I am especially angry
they flash like a switchblade,
foolish, but fierce,
and infinitely useful.

The Return of the Subjunctive

THE NORMAN INVASION

The Normans landed in Britain
in pointy shoes and floppy hats,
unpacked their rich cloth bags
of ornate Latinate words and speech,
and the island would never be the same.
Where once a man might simply think
he now could also *cogitate*;
where he once looked and watched
he now learned also to *observe*.
He no longer simply talked or spoke
for he could now also *discuss*, *dispute*,
debate, *converse*. To eat was no longer
a simple affair as the English learned
not just to chew but as well to *masticate*,
ingest and therefore to create *excrement*—
feces to later *defecate*—all this
when there used to be only one short word,
both noun and verb! And thanks
to the randy Normans, the island women
soon learned to *copulate*, *fornicate*
and have *intercourse* when all those crude
and lazy English men would ever learn
to do was fuck.

DONE

How do you know
when you're done?
After you've been stirred,
mixed, kneaded and left
to rise; after you've been rolled
flat and spread evenly;
after you've been sliced
and laid in concentric circles;
after you've been sprinkled
with love dust and crumbs;
after you've been covered
with other layers of yourself;
after you've been pinched
and pricked, placed
on the middle rack to heat
and stew and bubble
in your juices; you know
you are done
when a knife
inserted into your center
comes out clean.

THE STREAK

First we streaked the dean's house.
No one was home but we ran around it anyway
in tennis shoes and nothing else covering
our naked young bodies but night
(except for the boy in a kilt, too long even
for a giant, that he raised up so he could run
and show his stuff). We ran across campus

streaked Stork Tower hooting hollering
whooping at our mostly unnoticed antics.
We gathered ourselves into a circle
in the quad, arms across shoulders, dancing
the cancan or the hora or whatever it was
laughing, chanting, emboldened by beer
and cheered by marijuana. Later someone showed
the photos that they took for the school paper:

There was I, the only girl to face the lens,
my whiteness made shocking by that wedge
of pubic hair, and all the guys, penises soft
but pointing upward as caught by the camera
on the downward side of the hop as though
to say maybe they couldn't stop the war

or the draft or even the irresistible pull
of The System that would inevitably swallow
them whole, but they weren't gonna get hard
about it, that this was just a night to show
that we weren't afraid to take our clothes off
and have our pictures taken on a Saturday night

in Isla Vista, California, with the damp air sharpened
by eucalyptus and the gallons of oil that fouled
the shore, while the charred remains of the Bank
of America waited just off campus for the students,
the nation, to forget all the fuss and in fact
to join them when they got back to the business
of chewing up the world.

THE RETURN OF THE SUBJUNCTIVE

Oh, the Subjunctive,
May it make its bold return!
May it ride back proud
In liveried coach,
May its two fine horses snort
And paw the ground,
And, escorted by its staunch
Attendants If and Whether,
May it descend in velvet cloak
And black-gloved hand
The lacquered steps of hope
And happenstance.
May it fix upon us its deep
Uncertain gaze!
I shall be there to greet it
Though my company
Be small and moody.
I shall beg it stay
And may its presence give
Some respite from the steely glare
Of Indicative, a mantle to shield us
From Passive's clammy chill.
May it light again the land
Between the world that was
And is, and that which still might be,
And may we tread again desire's
Leaf-dappled path
Of possibility.

DOORS

Close the door, they tell her,
and another one will open.
She doesn't trust that advice
so she cheats and leaves the door ajar.
Wind rushes down the corridor
blowing leaves and wrappers,
the smell of the sea first
and after that, a swamp. It's cold.

She peers down the hallway—musty;
the closed doors stare like faces
with no features, like the backs
of spoons. A gust slams the door
ushers in a clutter of leaves and bits
of paper. "Looks like fall,"
he says, adjusts his glasses
and turns the volume up.

He doesn't notice the debris
that has blown in around his feet.
Soon he'll be asleep, mouth open;
she'll be out stalking the corridor
nightgown stuck to her legs
rushing past all the closed doors
to the waiting sea, the bright moon
pulling her toward the water.

LAY

You lay with me in emerald grass
While sunlight played and fireflies slept,
You laid your coat on the slippery mat
We lied and loved and lay and wept.

In slippery grass I drank your lies
Like nectar in the garden's May;
I licked my own lies from your lips
But that was when we lied and lay.

In liquored nights you lie with her
In sweaty grass on an emerald hill;
You lay her down on your coat of wool
And lie to her as she knows you will.

The grass lies bent, the flowers bruised
In the glossy field of waving rye
Your lips and ears aswarm with words
And almost every one a lie.

She cannot hear how you lied to me
How you laid your coat, how the flowers bent
How we lay together near the leper tree
Before our love arose and went.

You'll come again to this grassy place
To lie behind an April rain
And by September lying still
This is the play you will have lain

Loved and lied and laid and lain
Again, again, again, again.

CIRCE PLANS

First, I shall build myself
some new breasts:
great big globes,
hard shiny cannonballs
to punch guys in the eye.
These breasts will transfix
the tit men, beguile those
who like to say they prefer
legs, feet, ass,
but won't be able
to resist the gravity
of my invincible breasts
which won't move when I move,
age when I age, or die
when I die (which of course,
I never will).

These breasts will be Eternal.
I shall equip them
with tractor beams
that will shoot from the nipples
and drag men to me.
I'll fit them with guns
that fire at my will—
darts, BBs, blood-filled pellets,
or little flowers, the kind that burst
from a magician's gun—yes!—
that open on impact to release
a balm that will make men
abandon war, wealth, religion—
that will make them want
to spend their days
lazing in the fields,
admiring clouds
and cavorting with sheep,
while the women set about
making everything right.

ONE

If one were the only subject pronoun
one could use then one would have
a difficult time saying ordinary things.
One would have to be less direct,
one would have to beat, so to speak,
around the bush.

One would be safer, less exposed
for one could voice one's opinions
as though one's opinions belonged
to someone else: "One thinks
that too strong a metaphor," or
"One wishes that car would get off
one's ass." Or even "That dress
does make one's butt look big."

There would be no more accusations:
One would say instead, "Why did one leave
the back door unlocked?" or
"It seems one has forgotten to pay
the electric bill although one was reminded
to do so," or "Not tonight, dear, one has
a headache."

With all other pronouns made extinct,
one would speak easily in imperatives—
"Shut up!" "Sit down!" and, in fact,
"Please hand over that gold-plated pearl-
handled seven-bladed pocket knife
before one calls the cops on one's ass."

The world will be simpler then, without
the likes of You or Me or They who,
when you think about it, have caused
this world an awful lot of senseless
time-wasting confusion with statements
like "He's hitting me!" and the greatest
trouble-maker of all, "I love you."

REGRET

I don't invite her in.
She sits on the front porch
in a slim black dress with tight long sleeves
a hat with a veil in dotted swiss
and black kid gloves that she does not remove.

I can hear her shift sometimes in her seat
on the little wood bench out there, smell
her perfume like thousands of dead flowers
mixed with the odor of something else,
something that does not occur in nature.
Sometimes she smokes, cigarettes
of some defunct brand that she grinds out
on the porch boards with a two-inch stacked
pump heel.

After a while she leaves.
I hear her heels click on the concrete
and on down the street. Often
I don't hear her leave, forget about her
for weeks, months. Then she's back: the smoke,
the sad perfume, the shifting of her bony butt
on the hard porch seat, her skinny throat
scraping clear. I'm never letting her in.

She can sit out there forever
with her calendar, her long-handled mirror
that she keeps like a knife in the open purse
on her unhappy lap.

When she's out there I just move on.
I always use the back gate now.

RHETORICALLY SPEAKING

Oh, *apostrophe*, how would we know
you were not the mere sliver-moon
dangling between letters if our children
were not learning about you in school?

And *litotes*, not exactly obvious,
we would have thought you to be
a childhood chum of Socrates or Eurypides,
we are that ignorant. And if we are so dumb

why do our kids have to learn words
like *hypophora?* I mean, who talks like that?
Their teachers, maybe, and they're dumb too
or they wouldn't be teachers; they'd be stock brokers

or doctors of NBA stars or Swedes. Maybe
they study these words (which of course
they forget right away because they'll never
use them) so they can pass tests that show

not what they know but what the school tries
to cram into their skulls so their scores
might be high enough to keep the (*metaphorical*)
wolf from the school house door and of course

all American people should learn that fuck
is not the only *expletive*, clearly, of course,
don't you know, and that *metonymy*
by any other name would sound as sweet.

I'LL GIVE YOU RED

I'll give you red,
the color the Russians loved
so much they used it to make
their word for beautiful:
krasniy.

I'll give you scarlet
from the epaulets of blackbirds.

Or cardinal
from the spirits threading
through a steamy green
Midwestern afternoon

I'll give you crimson
from the feathers the parrot
hides in his tail
and only lets us see
when he is furious.

Here is your cerise
the sad, shameful stain of cherries.

And vermilion
the bright sash of yesterday
that lingers on the horizon.

I'll give you ruby
the color of lies
that lovers tell themselves,
the flame at the prism's
deepest heart.

But I will keep this red
the drunken sweet damp scent
of the breeze that sweeps
over strawberry fields
in June.

TAILLESS

I miss my tail,
still see it in my mind
twitching—no, swaying—
provocatively, on the sidewalk.
It will forget me
find another stump
make a new attachment.
I'll wander tailless
for a while, lighter;
it's easier taking corners
this way but still, it's a shock
at times, like combing your hair
after a drastic haircut;
you scrape your neck for days
but your head feels free
in its new nakedness.
After a while I'll start hunting
a new tail, try a few on
    twitch, twitch
keep one for a while, see
how well it corners,
lug it around
for too long after.
By then I'll be too old
to fit a new one.
I'll have to live
with this other, tired tail.
Sometimes I'll miss
my old one, the one I left
on the pavement
this morning,
the one with the diamond
pattern, iridescent houndstooth
gold threads invisible
to casual eye, threads
that match mine
exactly.

THE FARMER

The Latin professor rises
from his dusty bed,
the murmur of dawn
hums at his window.
In the gray light
he finds his glasses
puts on flannel pants
mouse-fur sweater, shoes
the color of sand dunes.
He gathers up his instruments:
pens, pencils, the leather-
bound volume of Cicero
and sets out into morning's
blush to till the tidy rows
of his fields: nominative
genitive, dative, ablative,
vocative, accusative...
Tenderly he irrigates
the verbs and their several
voices, prunes the budding
declensions, plants seedlings
in the fresh-turned soil.
I waken in my dusky
dream of Latin to find
my own mind's loamy rows
sprouting with new green
shoots that salute the sun
in Russian.

SAUDADE

*[sau'da-dji]—Portuguese. A feeling of longing for something
which is gone, and probably won't—but might—return.*

Saudade.
Now I get it,
this ache like hunger
only more painful
when you can't stop
thinking of that last meal:
how bright the salad,
crisp the crust
tender the bread,
tangy and full
of juice the meat, and how
you will never taste
that meal again.

Saudade
the way the last time
or the first time
remains in your mind
and you go over and over it
as your tongue worries
a sore tooth: the look,
the embrace, the kiss,
the sweater you wore
that lies ever folded
in your drawer, the letter
you never lose track of.

Saudade
This twist in the stomach
because that's the place
where love punched through
saying, here, here's this hole.
I'm leaving now
deal with it.

ESL CLASS

Driving down Sunset
The radio catches Vietnam
Its language bounces
Like a handball
Against a wall. The voice
Gives a local address:
The English glares like neon.

In my classroom students wait—
Their voices climb the dark
And complex scaffolding
Of several Slavic tongues.
Weaving through them:
The bright black beads of Spanish
Persian with its jeweled vines
The springy metal coils of China
Ethiopia's language of bone and seed

The sounds scatter
And fall like leaves
As I begin to teach
My language of aluminum.
The students try on new words
Like a costume awkwardly altered
A shaky structure bedecked
With beads, vines
Rubber balls bouncing.

A Little Life

SALTSHAKER BRIDE

You stand at table's end all trim
in your dress of pleated glass
cinched with a silvery band,
hat and veil of dotted stainless steel.
How pure and full you are, and ready
with your once-rare gift.

In the college dining hall
we line you up—
an army of brides—
and send you flying
down dining table aisle.
Your glass skirt unperturbed,
not one grain escapes the prim cap,
the crystal white of your dress.

You move toward your new life,
erect and proud, as momentum
sweeps you off the table,
suspends you for a moment
                                    in mid air
stainless steel veil revealing
no surprise or fear as you plunge,
perfect, to the floor.
Even then, you do not break.

We laugh because you look absurd
in your upright bravery
right then, before you fall
but the girls among us feel
a strange stirring as we stare
at the battleground
of fallen brides pert
in pretty dresses of pleated glass.

A LITTLE LIFE

My sister gently tosses
across our double bed a tiny
gray ball of fur that I catch and then
carefully toss back. We laugh, amazed:
It's a little life! she marvels, A little life!
After a few more tosses we let it fall softly
to the mattress where it stands, shakes
its furry young self and scurries off
to find a place where we're not.

Now my sister's child harbors her own
little life: a tiny thing still
the size, perhaps, of a grapefruit seed?
A seahorse? A thimble?
That something so small could cause
such a storm! One day he says
Keep it, the next he says
with more conviction, It has to go.
She wants to save him, wants to do
as he would like, but the images,
the words her mother gave her
all those years have settled
like the kernel in her womb.

She wishes she were like the others
for whom this might have been
an inconvenience, a fork
in a road not taken. But all the time
her boyfriend frets and wavers
she knows what she has to do.
There will be no tossing
of this little life.

THE RANCH

"He looks good in a white shirt."
"She's going to be fat someday."
Two weeks later they were married,
before she had even thought to ask
what he had studied at Iowa State:
    "Agronomy."
Did that mean he was going to be a farmer?
"Honey, I will never put you on a farm."

So nine years later when he came
through the door with an ecstatic smile
on his suntanned face her heart fell
into her stomach. "Honey," he said,
"I've bought some land."

They worked that plot of sand
planted baby orange trees and lemons
bought more land and planted trees
on that sand, too and he pumped
every ounce of feeling he had first
into that land and those trees.

He still looked good in a white shirt,
though she never got fat,
and as he promised he never did
put her on a farm: for all that time
until he died and she sold the land
and tractors plowed up
all the blossoming trees
everyone called that farm
the Ranch.

GARBAGE DAY

He'd roll out of the cab
a bear in black parka
wool cap, rounded thighs
in several pairs of pants
galoshes no matter what
the weather.
His face would open up
the smile a big slice
of cantaloupe
in the darkness of his face
and he'd be reaching out
for the boy's tossed ball
with palms as warm and bright
as candlelight.
Every week he'd stop
his busy rounds—hefting
dumping, putting back
the noisy, empty garbage cans—
to toss a ball
with the little blond boy
who had no brothers
no playmates
no parents, it often seemed
until one day
a tall man with angry eye
came striding fast
from the bus stop
told the boy to get inside
Now! and told him never
ever again, to play
with that nigger.

HIATUS

I don't go in my house.
Sometimes I go up to the door
peek through the hole
see the avalanche of mail
sun reaching in like a dusty ladder
but I don't even jiggle the lock.
Other times I wade through the side weeds
look through the windows
furniture still there
magazines piled on the table
but no, not yet.

When I am ready some day
I will turn the key in the lock
shoulder open the door
put my stuff down.
I'll go into the kitchen
get down a glass
turn on the faucet.
It's going to honk and wheeze
like a ghost that's dying
and nothing will come out at first
but some rusty sputum
as it honks and wheezes again
but then it will come
the water, and I'll let it run
for a while, staring
into the sink of old dishes.
I'll fill my glass
take a drink—not bad
could be better but hey—
and wonder
what took me so long.

WHAT A BEAUTIFUL VIEW, SHE SAYS

Outside my kitchen window
a liquidambar balances in leafy
arabesque, a jacaranda drops
its sticky-siren blossoms
onto the lawn and birds dance
on the grass beneath a redwood tree.
What a beautiful view! she says
again. I agree, tell her I am glad
that I don't have to take care
of it myself. Moments pass, we sip
our coffee and then, looking out
the window as if for the first time
she says it again: What a beautiful
view! She notices the view
every two minutes for at least
an hour, each time as delighted
as the time before.

One weekend she keeps saying,
How did you two meet? We tell
the story time and again, she listens
with interest, asks questions
for clarification, moments pass
and then she asks again
How did you two meet?
Another time her question is, When are you
getting married? She asks it
and asks it, he doesn't know what
to tell her. Tell her we already
did, I suggest later, ask her
Doesn't she remember? Sometimes

she asks about her brother.
They tell her he's been gone
for ten years now. Each time
it's a new blow to the stomach, a new

knife to the heart. When her daughter
dies, they don't know what to tell her.
Where is Barbara? she often asks.
She's coming, they tell her.
You'll see her. She misses you.

THE OWL AND I

The owl calls from the shadows
of the liquidambar tree.
I wonder what kind of thing
he's telling me—of his dark
and private hunger, of his scorn
for others and his longing?
He is looking for a lover
in the milky moonlight
but is sure he will not
find her, he with his swiveling
neck, his jowls, his stare.
There. He calls again.
I will go to him. He will
love me, I will ask
no questions. He will not care
that I am not an owl, that my head
no longer turns on my neck,
that my feathers come
from the discount store
or that I donate my gold
and silver hairs to the birds
each spring that they might weave
nests for their young, the babies
the owl and I will never have.

IMPASSE

In moonlight I wake
in the cold of our bed
too anchored to dreaming
to look for the blanket

I travel the mounded plain
between our bodies
and find you rising there
a far dark mountain

Asleep, your skin
is cool as the sheets
cool as the gulf
between us

When we wake
we touch arms
yours a dark fence, heavy
holds me in my place

Somewhere above
this gray morning landscape
of plain and mountain
our spirits entwine

like ribbons of smoke
and rising, do
what our bodies
no longer will

ABOUT YOU

You are right.
It is all about you
after all. Everything
is about you:

The words on everyone's lips
are about you.
The dog's bark
is about you.

The tree holding out its shade
and dropping blossoms
is about you.

The news we read
and especially the news
we watch is, in one way
or another, about you.

There is nothing
in this restless, damned world
that is not about you.

Even I and all that I think
and feel, though I have denied
it all this time,
am really about you.

So there you have it.
Take it back to your cave
and chew on it.

I made it for you.

BIG DICK

He liked to stand in front of the mirror
swaying side to side, waving it around.
He spoke to it fondly; fully clothed
it was always there—you had to see it
even if you didn't want to look.

It ruled him like a harridan, made him need
to stand out in a crowd, talk loudly,
be the fulcrum of every conversation.
It made him need to attract the sanctimonious
who would argue with him, and bullies
who would badger him briefly, then run away
sensing his genital superiority.

Sometimes he rode it like a bronco,
A Man and His Dick, heading out
for adventure, set to lead the weak
through the valley of darkness, conquer
the meek, beguile the fawning.
He would lead it like a horse to water,
and he loved to watch it pee.

Like a perfect pair of Siamese twins
they roamed the earth together,
too big for some to give pleasure
but destined to prevail in every situation.
In the absence of true friendship
and other companions, and until life
took its autumn turn,
they always had each other:

Big Dick with his gangling arms,
his superhero stride, and his ever-eager
good-old-boy, dangling-in-the-doorway
Dick.

THE BELLY REMEMBERS

Nobody cares about a thin person's belly.
Flat, even concave, a smooth surface
for a place setting, a writing table,
a cutting board. Not something rounded
and inviting like a hip.
Not something you just have to touch,
alive beneath your palms.
Not a cozy cushion
to lay your head against.
In silhouette, it is a vacant place,
a vacuum, a zero. So what
if it was once full with child,
if it swelled under a sweater,
a verdant hillside,
if it pushed out the navel like a headlight
on a locomotive,
if it gradually fell back later
like punched-down dough?
It was back to its stingy ways soon enough,
taut and smooth like a face with no features.
It's only when you sit that the skin puckers
and the places where it was once full
roll upon themselves in little waves
a series of pouting lips that tell you
what the belly remembers:
I, too, have housed a life.

BIG MOUTH

I keep my mouth wide open
tongue unfurled
each new thought
rippling like a wind-tossed flag.
Before I even know it's there
an opinion darts from my mouth,
glances off the hard protected heads
around me, or lodges in soft,
new open ones, a queer
foreign object.

How I envy the elegance
of the thought unspoken,
the wisdom of the voice restrained;
savor those few proud moments
when I've calmly kept my thoughts
in check and felt the smile
of the Sphinx
on my unruly lips.

Why do I need to spout
my mind with such abandon?
Where could it possibly lead
that's good? Ideas jostle
behind my lips, my mouth
full of them as a seedy fig.
It seems I need to believe
one just might fall someday
on fertile ears, a lucky seed
sprouting something of value.

I'VE HAD TITS

I've had tits
Tits like swelling buds
Tits the shape of thorns
Tits borrowed from a dog
Tits like tents
Tits full with the moon
tilted to one side, brooding
Dreamy tits warm in sunshine
Cold tits, affronted by air conditioning
Tits smashed sideways by a bra
Tits played like radio dials by boys
Tits swelling with the seasons
Tits perched atop the wide drum of a stretched belly
Tits transformed overnight into footballs
Tits transplanted, tits in the way
Tits spouting, emptying, filling
Tits so full they could burst, broken fountains
Tits I carried like an alien's child on my chest
Tits at which a man cried from a passing bus:
"Hey mama, give me some milk!"
Proud, active mother's tits
Civic-minded handfuls, not jugs
Tits to nicely fill a bra
Temporary tits
Tits which lost their ripe aplomb
fell back down like tired balloons
brooded again to opposing sides
half-hearted
vestigial
tits.

YOUR OCEAN

I will follow your eyes
with my horizon
Buoy your gaze on my face
of shining coins
Send my scent to you
over motioning air
and my voice to you
in your dreams

I will lay my great body
before your darkness
Wear your swath of light
like a slick and shining stole
Gather you into the vast reaches of me
where there will be no sense
of fear or shame: I will rise

and bump against your docks
raise your vessels high up
on my tide, carry you sleeping deep
within my murmuring body;
with only the scrape of sand
and shell to wake you
my cool, dark hips will pull you
back to sleep

SWIMMER

I am brick-heavy
porous
useless as a log adrift.
Other swimmers slice around me
like sharks
in a white-blue
flashing world of prisms;
I am like an old shoe
laces lost
eyelets empty
tongue-flapping dumb
taking on water.

WHAT YOU KNOW

Your tongue flows over
the boulders of your teeth
and flutters in the wind like a man's tie

I follow in your trotting path
to watch from behind
your velvet ears flap

you tumble on your side
to snort and wiggle your golden body
in the scratchy grass

you wag your whole head
and grin when you come to greet me
your whip-like tail waving in arcs

your muzzle, grown gray
with the decade, is a man's
suede oxford shoe

because every moment for you
is a prelude to enjoyment
even now as we wait for life

to pour you back
into its sure-flowing stream
we move within the shadow

cast by the coming loss of you
I watch your ribs rise
and fall with your living

find comfort in the knowledge
that you store in the walnut-shaped
bump on your skull

where among all the things you know
is the best one: that if you wait long enough
something good will always come along.

Wild Domestic

TO A HORNWORM
I. Discovery

My green friend, this morning
as you raise your head up
to look at me with black dot eyes
from where I find you, clinging
to my tomato branch, I see
your three rows of—are they hands?
teeth? I shall call them raspers
your eight stocky legs that hold tight
to the branch that you match
so perfectly it is hard to find you.
I admire your white stripes
the tiny black spots beneath them
the red horn at your back.

When I first found you there
a pudgy green bus lurking
beneath a denuded branch
behind the half-sucked tomatoes
above the inky caviar of your droppings
I recoiled, horrified; I am sorry—
I'm a human. It's a natural reaction.

But how calmly
with such self-possession
you feasted on my tomato plants
as though you had planted
and cared for them yourself.
Alas, I have had such friends
who feel it fine to borrow my clothes
without asking, use my lipstick
lie in my sheets, fill in
my crossword puzzles
with wrong answers, in pen.

A flitting shadow softly darkens
the once lush vines—a cream-winged
spotted butterfly. Eat up, I tell you.
Gather up strength
for your strange journey ahead
from which you'll emerge
a great striped moth.

To a Hornworm
II. Love's Retreat

At first I admired you
how cunning of you to be
the same deep green
as the leaves you inhabit,
to have those tasteful stripes
of red and that jaunty horn
on your tail. But then
I saw how you had ravaged
my tomato plants.

I couldn't kill you; plucked you
instead from your leafy perch
and flung you first
onto the grass, then
when you refused to go away
I hurled you onto the steaming
asphalt, a few warm red orbs
thus saved from your rapacious
teeth, but you kept coming back.

Now I hunt you down,
turn over every leaf, inspect
each stem. Now I see
how winsome you are at first,
a little green thread far smaller
than a stem. I pull you right off
the leaf and crush you
under my shoe. I find you
when you're older, not yet
a little green bus but nearly so
and I tear you off that ruined leaf
and smash you into the dirt.
I can now say that I know
how you would look
if you were jam: mint green
and spreadable.

WILD DOMESTIC

When it rains, the cats come in
to claim the comforts
of their entitlement:
spending days and nights curled
on a warm bed, doing nothing
while the dog, who only wants
to know them, paws at the door.

Raindrops swarm on the roof
the soaked ground sucks
at our footsteps. The cats lie about
entwined, too old now
even for the dinosaur dance
the fight game of their youth.
They nibble at their tinned prey
and even condescend
to use the litter box.

One black morning
they decide there's something
they need to do out there;
they scratch at the door and scurry out
into the shifting scrim of rain.
I drive home later to find
the wilder one, the one with crooked tail
waiting by the door—a bird clenched
motionless in his mouth.

He will not suffer my appreciation
hurries instead to his garage
encampment. This is the work
of wild things, which I need not know about.
Inside, the dog who only wants
to know them, listens
head cocked, at the door.

TIGER

The tiger must know
I am so afraid
but all the same
I want him

for the tiger
is the most beautiful
of all the wild things.

He could snap my neck
in the catch of a breath,
bury his face
in my steaming insides.

For a while
I would sustain him.
But would he love me
even then?

If we met in my dreams
I would rest
on the rumbling tide
of his sleep.

He would be gentle.
I could sleep there.
The moon would be bright
on the yellow grass hills.

AT DUSK

The heron waits in new grass.
A young dog for whom life
is an endless reel of joy
and desire bounds forward
to the strange new vision
near the pines.

The great bird stands
neck stretched out
like the beak of a tall urn
still as a vase
until the last moment
when the golden roiling
dog-body reveals
its fervent canine grin.

The bird slowly opens
its huge slate wings
and, reluctant, mounts
the heavy air
just above the tallest grass
barely out of the dog's reach
and sails, unhurried,
to the harbor
of a golf course pond.

The dog buries its muzzle
in a hole; an orange moon
pauses soft over the trees,
a tired balloon.

ANIMAL

I love the animal in you
the warm fur of your haunches
your tender underbelly
the soft bass of your heartbeat
your growl and your purr

I love the feral fighter in you
that can snap a neck and shake
the limpened body like a toy,
that can wrest if it must
the crimson viscera
from its fang-torn housing

I love the mother in you
and the father who can call
the frightened young
to your heart with one kind
motion and remind it that life
can be a loving and a safe place
like the cushioning womb
of the human in you.

ACCEPTANCE SPEECH
for Bolsa Chica

Blackbirds, thank you for that one harmonica
note in your song, for your scarlet shoulders
livening the yellow grass.

Mustard rising up taller than a man
thank you for your yellow
bright against the gray of spring.

Thank you snake, cooling in green shadow
for your explicit warning.

Vulture flushed from brushy haunt
thank you for your tender underwing
as you rise up to your dead branch perch.

Swallows stitching above marsh grass
thank you for your tawny bellies.

Thank you radish, growing wild your flowers
lavender and white, for your spicy pods.

Heron sailing to the clamor
in your enormous nest, thank you
for your noisy children.

Kids with paintball staining dirt, bikes
soaring over mud moguls, dusty faces
for my dog to lick, thank you
for the treehouses you hammered
onto the unpruned branches.

Thank you place for being wild:
dog shit dirt road, eucalyptus dying and alive,
pale branch like a desperate hand
reaching from the oily swamp.

Until they pave these roads
fence off the winter ponds, plant
only native plants and lock out all of us,
thank you for taking me among your number,
for letting me be like you, almost native,
almost wild.

MOUNTAIN ANTS

Up here the sky
is a thin blue skirt
the dusty summer sunlight
smells of woodsmoke
and pine
and ants grow big
and black as berries.

I watch them follow
their secret trails
in the fine mountain dust,
envy their purpose
and their path, wonder
at their sturdy black bodies,
imagine a breakfast
of ant jam.

INTO OCTOBER

Into the orange, orangutan world
into the woods' free greening
into the thick enamel snow
of egret feathers winging

like a spear I throw myself
into sleep's deep mirror
into the cool blue skirts of waves
into the darkness nearer

into the deep of voices
into a forest teeming
I brush aside the branches, fall
into the leaves of dreaming.

MALIBU FIRE

A red boil rises
in the eastern sky to show
a film of ash on asphalt:
your wedding photos
your tax returns, the couch
you could not get rid of.

Like a timid snowfall
the flakes sift down:
your closets full of clothes
for each of your changing sizes;
a decade of newspapers stored
in neat columns in your spare
garage; a marriage full
of Christmas ornaments.

When the wind is right
the sky shows its shy blue face
until the smoke returns
bringing with it your law books,
your socks, your brand new
king size bed.

Flames glitter on the hillside:
This is something big,
they tell us. We are stronger
than you will ever be.

And they bring us their booty:
all those ancient phone books
the magazines you had no time
to read, the Bible you held
at confirmation, your mask
and snorkel, your careful
landscaping, and plastic,
all that plastic.

LITTLE GREEN THING

Like a tiny armored vehicle, you rove
the hay-colored field of my coffee table
bedraggled little green thing, no one
can tell me your name but your bright
copper eye startles and repels me
as I watch you climb into my milk
and I take you with the cup, leave you
outside where it is newly spring
and the air is cold. At first
I don't understand that the case
you drag behind you like an empty
bullet shell is the place where
you were born just now, that the bags
you carry oddly furled at your sides
are lacy green wings, as new and wobbly
as your awkward young self, that soon
will open and bear you away;
you will know exactly where to go
right then, without even a thought
and I'll go back to my labyrinth
of could be, what if, and was.

THE HOUSEGUEST COOKS A MEAL

This morning I saw her
say her daily prayers,
breathing in her fragrant calm.
Now she stands
like a lush plant
in a green silk sari
about to bestow a blessing
on my kitchen.
But in this house
the brown rice has sat
unused for so long
that when she opens the jar
we see that inside the glass
tiny black bugs dance
among the grains of rice.
I am embarrassed
but she smiles, takes a bowl
from the shelf
and empties the jar.
I watch her careful hands
gently pluck small bugs
like cracked peppercorns
and place them on a plate.
When all the precious
insect lives are safe
she sets the plate outside
and smiles, rinses the rice
several times and makes a meal
of vegetables, spices
and clean brown rice.

The Radiance

DROP DEAD!

You spat it out like venom
at your playground enemy
and it felt so good to say
Drop dead! Late in life

it becomes a sweet mercy
to imagine: one minute
you're treading the earth
as ever, the next you're gone!

No hospitals, MRIs, CAT scans,
surgery, no loved ones
standing around wondering
if you're still breathing

and what to do with you
in case you are. And though
I'll never be ready for you to go,
as long as it is your wish

to leave this way, it is mine.
And may it happen on a day
when you are singing with friends,
laughing at a joke, dancing

in your living room.
May it come to you before
you know it and you'll find
yourself flying, a balloon

cut loose, taking one last glance
at this fond world that you have loved.
Though it will feel so cold to us,
this world without you, still

with all my heart here is my wish
for you dear friend, mother,
kindred soul: when the time comes,
Drop dead!

LAST LIGHT

Gravity is our first home,
our front yard,
our street, our mothers
calling us back,
the encircling arms
that we push against.

We are dancers
and it is the floor
that our feet caress
and defy.

It is our tether
holding us safe
as we ignore it
to explore our sky.
When we grow tired,
it rocks us with our own dreams.

Later, it pulls us harder:
our hair, our skin,
our bones strain away
from it, fall toward it.

Some stand tall
against its tireless effort,
letting sleep be just a small
concession, a sweet
delay, a preview;

Others race to it,
to the chair, the couch
and finally the bed
and that moment

When the earth pulls us
into its final dark embrace,
our last light.

LAX, 9/12/2001

Silent, spellcast:

Jets stuck still
like empty carcasses
of spiders dead,
ladders clinging
to their sides
like webs
abandoned

Air
that lately churned
with engines roaring
now quiet
as a lullaby.

Even the streets
have lost
their purpose;
they stretch,
vacant entrails,
over silent ground.

And the sky so still,
so blue!
No single chunk
of metal crowding
cloud or bone or feather.

For days this new
enchantment holds:
the world watches
as a great nation recoils
stunned dumb
to waken
three days hence

And reel at last—
avenging Cyclops,
blinded, raving,
bawling—from its cave.

IF YOU DIE IN YOUR SLEEP

If you die in your sleep
perhaps you dream
your moorings loosen,
feel your true ship thump
against the dock

become a balloon,
weights thrown aside,
ropes cut, bumpy at first
then deftly mounting
the sky's blue eye

soar high over
the green-patch fields
of the living, your own shadow
a small black fleck
edging the horizon

wake from that dream
and thread yourself like smoke
among the lives of your living
and see, at last, what was going on
all that time.

Perhaps they feel you brush
the soft armhairs of awareness,
inhale the comfort
of your spirit breath.

As you glide away
perhaps they tell themselves
of course it was not you,
was only the longing
for you, the keen yearning
to say goodbye again.

THE RAPTURE

How I envy
the furry black
yellow striped
caterpillar
that climbs
the lush stems
of the basil plants.
Sheltered within the deep
green redolent canopy
it spends its days
feasting
on the fragrant leaves,
unaware
that with each
delicious bite
it destroys
its gorgeous habitat.
By the time the leaves
are all reduced
to lacy stubble
it will be time
to find a resting place,
pull a shroud over itself
and wait for the dawn
of the next life.
How I envy
the furry black
yellow striped
caterpillar
that can destroy
its world
and retreat
to the succor
of a regenerative
cocoon.

ON THE LOSS OF AN ONLY CHILD

Afterward
she pulled the grief
like a long rope
out of her—
a thick twisting cable
made of muscle,
   of blood,
   of flesh
   of suffering,
   of love—
a sturdy artery
like the one the doctor
pulled from her
when the baby was born
but this one had no end,
it just kept coming out.
Long after the river
which flowed
storm-swollen
through her
had slowed
to a rusty vein,
long after all the sharpest
pain of loss had calmed,
the grief kept circling
like that rope
in milky coils around her
until she could not see over it,
could not step out of it,
could not move beyond it.
Only a slender straw
of light pierced through
and this light, too,
was a memory.

IT WORKED

Oppenheimer Recalls the Bhagavad Gita
July 16, 1945

In the dim and quiet pre-dawn light
a few streaks of gold tint the eastern
sky over Alamogordo, New Mexico.
Then, to pierce the quiet and the dim,
bursts the brightest light
that has ever been in the time of man

a light that blasts, pounces, and bores
its way through all who see it, a light
you feel with your whole being,
a colossal ball of fire swelling, rising,
rolling, a huge blazing snowball
climbing the sky in screaming yellow
scarlet, green, a light whose awful

brilliance shadows all who watch
that day and all of those who live
thereafter. This is the radiance
of a thousand suns, the scientist thinks,
the splendor of the Mighty One, Death,
the shatterer of worlds.

THE BODY OF GOD

Form is emptiness, emptiness is form. Heart Sutra

Cold tile beneath bare feet
They say you are made mostly
Of space
Cool mud beneath the blades of grass
You too, and your grass sticking up
Are mostly space
They say that space is everywhere
That we part it with our bodies
Yet still it fills us
That it is why we are humming
With life, that even sitting still
Like this oaken table
We are not merely taking up space
But are infused with it
That no matter what we do
Or think or feel
There is no getting out of this
We are forever filled with this space
And this space is God
So God is all around and in us
And all of us forever dwell
In the body of God.
For some of us
That is all we need to know.

TAMARA MADISON grew up on a citrus farm near Mecca, California, and began writing poetry as soon as she could hold a pen; her first publication was a poem which appeared in a local newspaper when she was twelve. Her chapbook *The Belly Remembers* won the Jane Buel Bradley prize in 2004 and was published by Pearl. Tamara is a graduate of Georgetown University, with a BS in Linguistics. She now teaches French in a public high school in Los Angeles.